FUNGI POWER

FUNGI as FOOD

CHERRY LAKE PRESS
Ann Arbor, Michigan

by Joyce Markovics

Cherry Lake Press

Published in the United States of America by
Cherry Lake Publishing Group
Ann Arbor, Michigan
www.cherrylakepublishing.com

Reading Adviser: Beth Walker Gambro, MS, Ed., Reading Consultant, Yorkville, IL

Content Adviser: David S. Hibbett, PhD, Clark University, Worcester, Massachusetts

Book Designer: Ed Morgan
Book Developer: Bowerbird Books

Photo Credits: © Ed Morgan, cover, title page, and table of contents; © EkaterinaSid/Shutterstock, 4–5; © freepik.com, 5 bottom, 6; © Philippe 1 bo/Shutterstock, 7; © Serg Zastavkin/Shutterstock, 8; © MakroBetz/Shutterstock, 9; © Fotografiecor.nl/Shutterstock, 10; © milart/Shutterstock, 11; © freepik.com, 12–13, 14, 15, 16, 17, 18, 19 bottom; © Ermak Oksana/Shutterstock, 19 top; © Volodymyr Nikitenko/Shutterstock, 20; © freepik.com, 21; © Antonin Vinter/Shutterstock, 22; © Michael Siluk/Shutterstock, 23; © freepik.com, 24; U. Schmidt, 2014/Wikimedia Commons, 25; © freepik.com, 26–27; © krolya25/Shutterstock, 28; © Edwin Butter/Shutterstock, 29 top; John Maxwell for USFWS/Wikimedia Commons, 29 bottom.

Cherry Lake Press is an imprint of Cherry Lake Publishing Group.

Library of Congress Cataloging-in-Publication Data has been filed and is available at catalog.loc.gov

Printed in the United States of America

CONTENTS

ON THE HUNT

On a cool February day, **mycologist** Charles Lefevre trudges through an Oregon forest. By his side are his furry coworkers, Dante and Luca. Both are Lagotta Romagnolos, a dog breed from Italy. They are prized for their ability to sniff out buried treasure. Suddenly, Dante dives through a pile of branches. Charles runs after him. The dog stops and smells a patch of soil. Charles drops to one knee and grabs what looks like a big black nugget out of the soil. This is the treasure! It's a mushroom called a truffle.

Dante loves truffles as much as people do. "If I take my eyes off him for a second, he'll eat a truffle," Charles said. How did Dante find the knobby mushroom? Truffles have an intense **aroma**. The smell can be so strong that sometimes Charles can smell ripe ones buried in the soil. But Dante and Luca are the expert sniffers.

A Lagotta Romagnolo is known for being alert and intelligent, making it a great truffle hunter.

FUNGI Facts

Truffles are a kind of fungi (singular fungus). They come in different shapes, sizes, and flavors. The most desired and valuable are white truffles.

The dogs race through the forest. After a couple of minutes, they sniff out another truffle—and another. "Every time we come here, we find about $5,000 worth of truffles," said Charles. Many truffle hunters sell their haul to restaurants. The fungi can be made into oil, cheese, ice cream, and chocolate, or shaved on top of pasta and other dishes. But Charles donates his to a truffle festival he helped found. One of his goals is to celebrate truffles and educate people about them.

Black truffles can smell like damp forest soil with hints of garlic and pepper.

Pigs are sometimes used to hunt for truffles. However, they can rip up and damage the forest floor with their hooves and snouts.

Charles also has another passion. He helps plant truffle tree orchards! They are called *truffières*. To do this, Charles places truffle spores in the soil near the roots of certain trees. Spores are very tiny, seedlike particles that help fungi **reproduce**. Truffles grow in close connection with the roots of some trees. In doing this work, Charles helps replenish the truffles he has **harvested**. He also makes sure there are plenty for future **generations**.

FUNGI Facts

Truffles are among the most expensive foods in the world. Some can sell for hundreds of thousands of dollars!

Fungi Basics

Truffles are a delicious part of the fungi kingdom. Other fungi include yeasts, molds, and mildews. Fungi can be found almost everywhere on Earth. For hundreds of years, people thought fungi were plants. However, scientists later discovered that fungi are more similar to animals than to plants. How? They cannot make their own food. So, they must find it.

This inedible strawberries-and-cream fungus oozes a red liquid. It's also called the bleeding tooth fungus.

After a spore **germinates**, it grows into long, thin tubes called hyphae (HAHY-fey). The hyphae spreads through the soil, searching for **nutrients**. As the hyphae get longer, they branch out and fuse together. This living network is called mycelium (mahy-SEE-lee-uhm). As the mycelium grows larger and becomes more **entangled**, it produces cells that form spores. The spores are often contained within mushrooms. These are the fruiting bodies of some fungi, not unlike an apple on a tree. Certain mushrooms, like truffles, grow underground. That's why they have such a strong scent. They need animals to find them and spread their spores. Other mushrooms appear in places where people can easily see them, such as fields and forests.

Mycelium

FUNGI Facts

There are millions of kinds of fungi. Not all are edible, but many are!

Fungi, including truffles, have a special relationship with trees and other plants. Hyphae absorb water and nutrients from the soil. Trees create their own food. However, they sometimes struggle to absorb water and nutrients. This is where the hyphae can help. They latch onto the tree's roots and give the tree the water and nutrients it needs. In return, the tree provides the fungus with sugars it makes through **photosynthesis**.

An edible lion's mane mushroom growing on a tree

Through this relationship, fungi can make tasty mushrooms. Fungi are a food source for many living things, including animals and humans. Mushrooms aren't just yummy, they're also healthy. They contain protein, which builds muscle. Mushrooms are also a good source of vitamins B and D and minerals, such as **selenium**. Additionally, they are known to combat **inflammation** and have the potential to fight diseases such as cancer.

This jack-o-lantern mushroom looks like an edible chanterelle. However, it's poisonous.

FUNGI Facts

Not all mushrooms are safe to eat. Some are poisonous and can be deadly! NEVER PICK AND EAT WILD MUSHROOMS.

WHAT'S FOR DINNER?

Mushrooms are healthy. But they also taste good! They have a rich, savory flavor. It's sometimes described as umami (oo-MAH-mee). Umami is said to be the fifth taste, after sweet, sour, salty, and bitter. Mushrooms also have a distinct texture. Some people describe it as meaty. Mushrooms can be used to make burgers and tacos as well as soups and stews. Some of the most popular types are button, cremini, maitake, oyster, porcini, and shiitake.

Many of these fungi are grown on farms. They're one of the most **sustainable** foods because they require little water and space to grow. One acre (0.4 hectares) of land can produce up to one million pounds (453,592 kilograms) of mushrooms each year. Mushrooms, however, only make up a small part of the fungi that people eat. There are countless other foods made using fungi. Can you guess some? They're probably foods you eat every day.

FUNGI Facts

Mushrooms are farmed in all 50 states. However, the majority of mushrooms are grown in Pennsylvania.

Nothing smells better than freshly baked bread. Did you know that it's made with fungi? Baker's yeast is a type of fungus. When it's added to bread dough, it eats the sugars in the dough. Then it produces a gas called carbon dioxide. This process is called **fermentation**. The gas gets trapped in the dough, creating air pockets. This causes it to rise. The result is light, fluffy, mouthwatering bread.

A bowl of yeast bread dough

While yeasts are beneficial to bread-making, other fungi can be harmful. Have you ever seen fuzzy, green and white growths on bread? The culprit is bread mold. Mold spores are carried through the air. When they land on bread, especially if it's in a dark, moist place, they grow. The mold sends hyphae twisting throughout the bread. It also makes microscopic fruiting bodies. While most molds are not dangerous, some can make people sick. Remember to either **compost** moldy bread or toss it in the trash.

Bread mold

FUNGI Facts

Molds are helpful to people and the planet. They break down and recycle nutrients in the environment. Some are even made into life-saving medicines.

Other molds are used to make another one of the world's most popular foods—cheese! Not all cheeses are made with mold. But some of the most delicious kinds are. Blue cheese is one example. It's made from milk and *Penicillium roqueforti* mold. Where did blue cheese come from? Legend has it that a cheesemaker in France left a loaf of bread near some cheese. Over time, the bread developed mold. And the mold spread to the cheese. Then he tasted the moldy cheese and liked it.

Blue cheese got its name from the blue-green mold that grows in it.

Today, blue cheese is made in a more controlled setting. First, milk is mixed with special **bacteria** that change it from a liquid to a solid. Then **rennet** is used to separate the milk into curds or lumps. The curds are then formed into wheels. And mold spores are added. Finally, the wheel is poked with long spikes. This step allows oxygen to reach the mold, encouraging its growth. The result is rich, blue-green spots or veins in the cheese. "Cheesemaking is very physical, labor-intensive work," said Mike Thomson, a blue cheesemaker. But the result is unforgettably good.

A cheesemaker pours curds into a mold to shape the cheese into a wheel.

FUNGI Facts

There are several types of blue cheese, including Roquefort, Stilton, and Gorgonzola. The flavors vary from mild and creamy to pungent and crumbly.

For thousands of years, people in Asia have been using another mold to make flavorful foods. It's called *Aspergillus oryzae*, or koji mold. Without it, soy sauce and some other food favorites wouldn't exist. To make soy sauce, the mold is added to crushed soybeans and wheat. It "smells like a wonderful mix of mushroom and grapefruit, and a little bit sour as well," said **microbiologist** Benjamin Wolfe. The mold releases **enzymes**, which break down the soybeans and wheat. The mixture then ferments for several months. Lastly, it's strained to separate the liquid from the solids.

Soy sauce

Miso, a creamy paste, is also made using soybeans and koji mold. Known for its rich, savory flavor, miso can be used to make soups, dressings, and other dishes.

Tempeh is a **traditional** Indonesian food. It's often used as a meat substitute. How is it made? The fungus *Rhizopus oligosporus* is added to soybeans. Then they ferment. A thick mat of mycelium binds the beans together. The final product has a firm texture and nutty flavor.

Miso paste

Tempeh

Some **delicacies** include fungi as a star ingredient. *Huitlacoche*, also known as corn smut, is a gourmet food in Mexico. It's a fungus that grows on corn, causing the kernels to swell and turn purplish gray. Although it's a plant disease, it's valued as a food source. Sometimes called the "Mexican truffle," the fungus has a smoky and sweet flavor. It's added to dishes, such as quesadillas (kay-suh-DEE-uhz), tacos, and omelets.

Corn smut

Cocoa beans for making chocolate

Chocolate is another food enhanced by fungi. Without fungi, chocolate wouldn't taste the same. It would be too bitter to eat! Chocolate comes from the seeds of the cacao (kuh-KAY-oh) tree, which grow in pods. The seeds have a bitter outer coating. Yeasts, along with bacteria, break down the bad-tasting coating. Then the beans are dried and roasted. The result is the chocolaty flavor loved around the world.

FUNGI Facts

Citric acid is an ingredient in many foods. Made by a type of mold, it adds tartness to candy and sodas. It also keeps some food from spoiling.

Food for All

Fungi are food for more than just humans. Leafcutter ants live in huge **colonies** in forests. They use their powerful, chainsaw-like jaws to cut leaves. Then the tiny ants carry the leaf bits back to their sprawling underground nests. The leaves are food for the ants' fungus farm! That's right. Leafcutter ants are fungus farmers.

Leafcutter ants can carry pieces of leaves that are 50 times their own weight. That's comparable to a person lifting a car!

The fungus provides food for baby ants. In return, the ants feed the fungus with fresh leaf clippings. If the fungus doesn't like a particular plant the ant brings to it, the colony will stop collecting it. The ants also clean the fungus by removing pests and molds that might attack it. When both organisms benefit, the relationship is known as mutualism (MYOO-choo-uh-liz-uhm).

Above is a leafcutter ants' underground fungus farm. The nest can be 25 feet (7.6 meters) deep.

FUNGI Facts

Lines of foraging leafcutter ants can stretch 100 feet (31 m) long.

A termite mound

Leafcutter ants are not the only insects that farm fungus. Termites and ambrosia beetles are some others. Both have their own farming techniques. Some species of termites build large mounds that can reach heights of 10 feet (3 m). These nests maintain ideal growing conditions for fungi. Like leafcutter ants, the termites feed fungi with plant matter, such as wood and leaves. They also protect the fungi from pests. In exchange, the fungi provide food for the termites.

FUNGI Facts

Because of their unique design, termite mounds stay at a controlled temperature.

Ambrosia beetles make their homes in dead or dying trees. And when they find a new place to live, they bring fungal spores with them! The beetles carve out tunnels in the wood. After that, they deposit the fungus and lay eggs in the tunnels. The fungus eats the wood. After the baby beetles hatch, they munch on the fungus's mycelium. The adult beetles tend to the fungus, making sure it's free from anything that can harm it. The fungus depends on beetles to carry it to a new tree and food source. How's that for teamwork?

This is an ambrosia beetle. These tiny, reddish-brown insects are only about as big as the tip of a pencil. They can infest many kinds of trees.

LOOKING AHEAD

What's the future of fungi-based foods? Scientists are developing a boba-like fungi product called "myco-foods." It has the potential to feed a lot of people at a small cost. Fungi not only provide food for humans, insects, and other living things. They also help the planet. How? They recycle nutrients, enhancing the soil to help plants grow. Fungi also break down **pollutants** and prevent **erosion**. However, unless we protect the places where fungi live, they won't survive and there will be less food. "Our world is changing rapidly before our eyes," Heather Dawson, a scientist and truffle expert, said. "We're losing **diversity** as we speak."

How can we save the many fungi species and their plant partners? Humans can stop polluting the planet and destroying fungi habitats. If you cut down a tree, "you're also killing many of the fungi that live on those roots," said Heather. "We're going to end up losing a lot."

FUNGI Facts

Scientists believe there are millions of fungi species on Earth. However, 95 percent have yet to be discovered.

WHO KNEW? FUN-gi Facts

Spore Shocker

Fungi produce approximately 50 megatons (1 megaton equals 1 million tons) of spores each year. In total, the spores would weigh as much as 500,000 blue whales! Puffballs, a ball-shaped fungus, shoot their spores into the air when an animal or something else touches them. The spores look like a puff of smoke, which explains the fungus's name. Some spores rise high in the sky. There, they help raindrops form. Eventually, rainclouds are created. So, the next time it rains, say, "It's raining mushroom spores."

Ink Cap Mushrooms

These mighty mushrooms can push their way up through asphalt, or pavement! Also called lawyer's wig mushrooms, these funky fungi can also be eaten when they're young. However, once they turn black, they're no longer edible. Old ink caps eventually dissolve into a black liquid. People use this "mushroom ink" for writing and drawing!

Woodpecker Fungus Farmer

Red-cockaded woodpeckers make their homes in pine trees. And they prefer trees with conk fungus growing on them. Why? The fungus weakens the trees, making it easier for the woodpeckers to hammer through the wood to build their nests. Then the woodpeckers do the fungus a favor. They spread it to other pine trees! How's that for a mutually beneficial relationship?

GLOSSARY

aroma (uh-ROH-muh) a pleasant odor

bacteria (bac-TIHR-ee-uh) tiny life-forms that can be seen only under a microscope

colonies (KAHL-uh-neez) groups of animals

compost (KAHM-pohst) to turn vegetable matter and fungi into organic material used to grow plants

delicacies (DEL-ih-kuh-seez) foods that are rare and pleasing to eat

diversity (dih-VUR-sih-tee) the variety of life on Earth

entangled (en-TANG-guhld) twisted together

enzymes (EN-zahymz) substances that cause chemical reactions, such as digestion

erosion (ih-ROH-zhuhn) the wearing away of land by water, wind, or ice

fermentation (fur-men-TAY-shuhn) a chemical process in which something breaks down into simpler substances

generations (jen-uh-RAY-shuhnz) groups of people born around the same time

germinates (JUR-muh-nayts) begins to grow or develop

harvested (HAR-vuh-stid) collected by people

inflammation (in-fluh-MAY-shuhn) redness, pain, and swelling in the body often caused by injury or infection

microbiologist (mye-kroh-bye-AH-luh-jist) a person who studies microscopic organisms

mycologist (mahy-KAHL-uh-jist) a person who studies fungi

nutrients (NOO-tree-uhnts) substances needed by fungi and other living things to grow and be healthy

photosynthesis (foh-tuh-SIN-thuh-siss) the way plants make food using water, carbon dioxide, and sunlight

pollutants (puh-LOOT-uhnts) substances that decrease the quality of air, water, soil and food

pungent (PUHN-juhnt) having a sharp smell or taste

rennet (REN-it) a substance that comes from animal stomachs and is used to make cheese

reproduce (ree-pruh-DOOS) to make more of a living thing

selenium (sih-LEE-nee-uhm) a mineral that plays a key role in the human body

sustainable (suh-STAYN-uh-buhl) a way of living that does not use up or deplete natural resources

traditional (truh-DISH-uh-nuhl) long-established

LEARN MORE

BOOKS

Boddy, Lynne. *Humongous Fungus*. New York: DK, 2021.

Bonkoski, Ariel. *Mushrooms & Fungi for Kids*. New York: Adventure Publications, 2025.

Gravel, Elise. *The Mushroom Fan Club*. Montreal, Canada: Drawn and Quarterly, 2018.

WEBSITES

Explore these online sources with an adult:

Kids Britannica: Fungus
The Mushroom Council: Five Amazing Mushroom Facts for Kids
The Mushroom Council: Kid-Friendly Recipes
New York Botanical Garden: Fungi and Lichens
PBS Learning Media: Fungi

INDEX

ABOUT THE AUTHOR

Joyce Markovics has written hundreds of books for kids. She lives in an old house along the Hudson River. Joyce is fascinated by fungi and what we don't yet know about these extraordinary life-forms. She would like to dedicate this book to Finley, a young writer who appreciates the delicious things in life. Joyce also expresses gratitude to mycologist David Hibbett for his expertise and generosity in creating this book.